A Guinea Pig Nativity

A Guinea Pig Nativity

B L O O M S B U R Y

LONDON • NEW DELHI • NEW YORK • SYDNEY

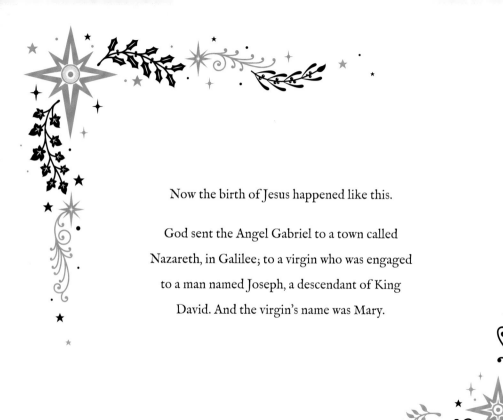

Now the birth of Jesus happened like this.

God sent the Angel Gabriel to a town called
Nazareth, in Galilee; to a virgin who was engaged
to a man named Joseph, a descendant of King
David. And the virgin's name was Mary.

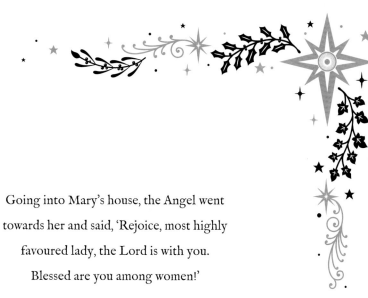

Going into Mary's house, the Angel went
towards her and said, 'Rejoice, most highly
favoured lady, the Lord is with you.
Blessed are you among women!'

Mary was greatly disturbed by these words, and wondered
what sort of greeting this was!

The Angel said to her, 'Do not be afraid, Mary, for you
have found favour with God. Behold! You will conceive
and bear a son, and you shall call him Jesus.

'He will be great, and will be called Son of the Most High.
The Lord God will give him the throne of his forefather
David, and of his kingdom there will be no end.'

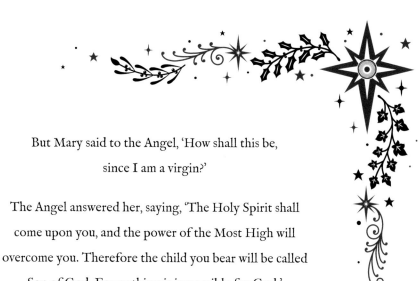

But Mary said to the Angel, 'How shall this be,
since I am a virgin?'

The Angel answered her, saying, 'The Holy Spirit shall
come upon you, and the power of the Most High will
overcome you. Therefore the child you bear will be called
Son of God. For nothing is impossible for God.'

Mary said, 'Behold, I am the handmaid of the Lord. Let it
be done to me as you have said.' And the Angel left her.

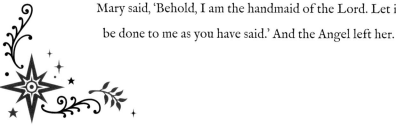

Joseph was an upright man; when he found out
that Mary was with child before they had married,
he was minded to avoid a scandal. He decided to
separate from her quietly.

Whilst he was brooding over these things, the Angel appeared to him during a dream and said, 'Joseph, Son of David, do not be afraid to take Mary as your wife, for the child she will bear was conceived by the Holy Spirit, and he will save the people from their sins!'

All this happened so that the words spoken by the Lord through the Prophet would be fulfilled: 'Behold, the virgin shall conceive, and bear a son, and they shall call him Jesus, which means "God is with us".'

When Joseph awoke from his dream, he did as the
Angel had told him and took Mary as his wife.

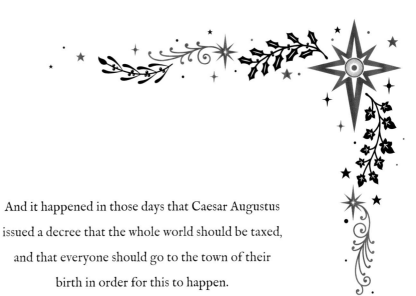

And it happened in those days that Caesar Augustus
issued a decree that the whole world should be taxed,
and that everyone should go to the town of their
birth in order for this to happen.

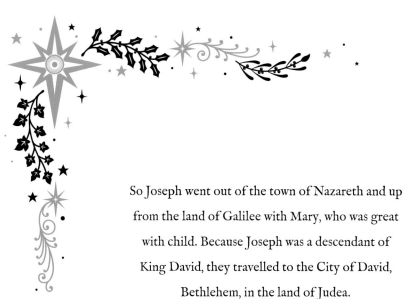

So Joseph went out of the town of Nazareth and up
from the land of Galilee with Mary, who was great
with child. Because Joseph was a descendant of
King David, they travelled to the City of David,
Bethlehem, in the land of Judea.

And so it came to pass that whilst they were in
Bethlehem, the time came for Mary to give birth.

And she brought forth her firstborn son, wrapped
him in swaddling clothes, and laid him in a manger –
because there was no room for them at the inn.

There were shepherds in the surrounding area, keeping their sheep and watching over their flocks by night.

And lo, the Angel appeared to them, and the glory of the
Lord shone around them. And they were very afraid!

The Angel said to them, 'Do not be afraid,
for I bring news of great joy for all people!

'For a Saviour is born for you this day in the City of David.
He is Christ the Lord! You shall find him wrapped in
swaddling clothes, and lying in a manger.'

Suddenly a multitude of the heavenly host appeared, praising God and saying, 'Glory to God in the Highest Heavens, and on Earth, peace to people of good will.'

As the Angels returned into Heaven the shepherds said to one another, 'Let us go to Bethlehem, and see this great thing that has happened, which the Lord has revealed to us.'

And they went with haste to Bethlehem, and found
Mary and Joseph, and the babe lying in a manger.

They then returned to the hills praising and glorifying
the Lord for all they had seen and heard; and all who
were told what the shepherds had seen were amazed.

But Mary kept all these things and
pondered them in her heart.

Now all this happened during
the reign of Herod the King.

And behold! Wise men from the East came to Herod, saying, 'Where is the King of the Jews? We saw his star rising in the East and have come to worship him.'

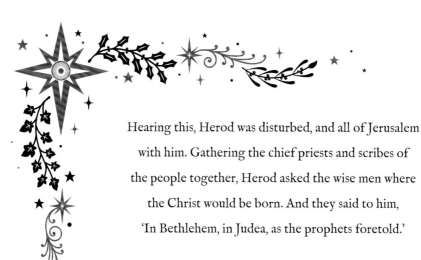

Hearing this, Herod was disturbed, and all of Jerusalem
with him. Gathering the chief priests and scribes of
the people together, Herod asked the wise men where
the Christ would be born. And they said to him,
'In Bethlehem, in Judea, as the prophets foretold.'

So Herod called the wise men to him secretly, and
asked them what time the star had appeared. He sent
them to Bethlehem, and said, 'Search carefully for the
child, and when you have found him tell me where he is,
that I may also come and pay him homage.'

After speaking with the King the wise men departed,
and the star that had appeared to them in the East
went before them, until it came and stood over
where the child was.

Seeing the star, the wise men were filled with great joy,
and when they saw the child with Mary his mother they
fell down before him, and worshipped him, giving him
gifts of gold, frankincense and myrrh.

But being warned by God in a dream that they should not go back to Herod, they returned to their own country by a different route.

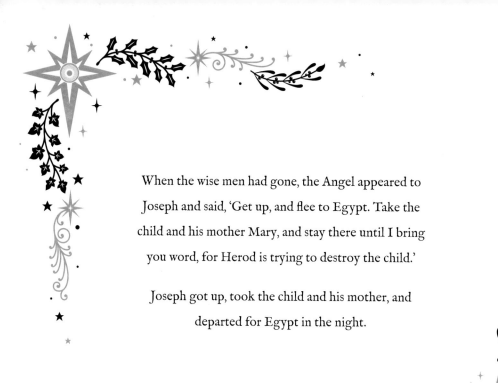

When the wise men had gone, the Angel appeared to Joseph and said, 'Get up, and flee to Egypt. Take the child and his mother Mary, and stay there until I bring you word, for Herod is trying to destroy the child.'

Joseph got up, took the child and his mother, and departed for Egypt in the night.

When Herod realized that the wise men had double-crossed him he was filled with rage.

He gave orders to slaughter all the infants in Bethlehem and the surrounding areas who had been born at the time the wise men had told him.

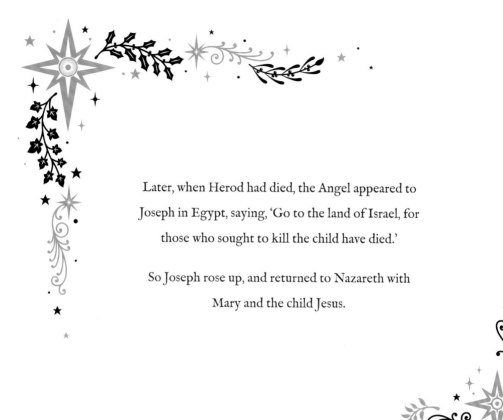

Later, when Herod had died, the Angel appeared to Joseph in Egypt, saying, 'Go to the land of Israel, for those who sought to kill the child have died.'

So Joseph rose up, and returned to Nazareth with Mary and the child Jesus.

And Jesus increased in wisdom and strength,

and found favour with God and humankind.

Dramatis Personae

The Angel Gabriel Maisie

Mary Wilma

Joseph Doris

Caesar Augustus Billie

First Shepherd Guinnea

Second Shepherd Molly

Third Shepherd Poppy

Herod the King Hollie

First Wise Man Evie

Second Wise Man Ellie

Third Wise Man Millie

The Baby

The publishers would like to thank Pauline, Amanda, Jen, Laura, Rachael and everyone who came with them for their patience, enthusiasm and brilliant sense of humour.

Small pets are abandoned every day, but the lucky ones end up in rescue centres where they can be looked after and rehomed. You may not know it, but some of these centres are devoted entirely to guinea pigs. They work with welfare organizations to give first class advice and information, as well as finding loving new owners for the animals they look after. This Christmas, share the yuletide spirit and perhaps think of supporting your local rescue centre!

Translation/text © D.M.

Photography © P.B.

Illustration © T.L.

First published in 2013

Bloomsbury Publishing Plc, 50 Bedford Square, London WC1B 3DP

Bloomsbury USA, 1385 Broadway, New York, NY 10018

www.bloomsbury.com

Bloomsbury Publishing, London, New Delhi, New York and Sydney

A CIP catalogue record for this book is available from the British Library.

Library of Congress Cataloging-in-Publication Data has been applied for.

UK ISBN: 978 1 4088 4479 3

US ISBN: 978 1 62040 587 1

10 9 8 7 6 5 4 3 2 1

All papers used by Bloomsbury Publishing are natural, recyclable products made from wood grown in well-managed forests. The manufacturing processes conform to the environmental regulations of the country of origin.

Design by P.B.

Printed and bound in China by C&C Offset Printing Co., Ltd.